BROKEN PROMISES

THE U.S. GOVERNMENT AND NATIVE AMERICANS IN THE 19TH CENTURY

The frozen body of a Lakota Sioux medicine man lies among the remains of the camp at Wounded Knee Creek, South Dakota. Someone has thrust a rifle into his clenched arms. In truth, almost none of the Indians were armed against the brutal surprise attack on December 29, 1890.

THE AMERICAN WEST

BROKEN PROMISES

THE U.S. GOVERNMENT AND NATIVE AMERICANS IN THE 19TH CENTURY

MIKE WILSON

MASON CREST PUBLISHERS

Mason Crest Publishers
370 Reed Road
Broomall PA 19008
www.masoncrest.com

 Printed and bound in the Hashemite Kingdom of Jordan.

First printing

1 3 5 7 9 8 6 4 2

Library of Congress Cataloging-in-Publication Data
on file at the Library of Congress

ISBN 1-59084-064-X

Publisher's note: many of the quotations in this book come from original sources, and contain the spelling and grammatical inconsistencies of the original text.

CONTENTS

At a time when the Native American cause seemed desperate, the prophecies of a mystic named Wovoka provided a new hope. The Ghost Dance ritual, the Sioux believed, would bring about a new world without white men and their broken promises.

1

THE GHOST DANCE

IN 1890, A SIOUX MAN NAMED WOVOKA BROUGHT A MESSAGE of hope to the Native Americans—the ghosts of dead Indians would rise and God would destroy the white man and create a new earth in which only Indians lived. Soon, the Indians of the Plains were calling Wokova a **messiah**.

Native Americans needed a message of hope. During the past 100 years the white men had tricked the Indians and taken their land, slaughtered them, and broken promises. They lured Indians to **parley** under the white flag of **truce**, and then captured or killed them.

First, Native Americans had been pushed to the west. Then, when the whites wanted that land, the Indians had been moved further west. Every time gold was discovered on Indian land, white men found a way to take the land, either by force or by trickery. When there was no place left to move the

Indians, the whites took their lands and confined them to small **reservations** that did not have enough game to feed their tribes.

People who once roamed freely throughout the continent now were prisoners on reservations, dependent on handouts from the U.S. government to survive. Often, the government promised food and supplies but did not give them. Native Americans were forced to give up their religion and told to adopt the ways of the white man.

But now Wovoka said that Indian ghosts would rise if the Indians did the "Ghost Dance." In a matter of months, Native Americans throughout the West were dancing in brightly colored shirts printed with pictures of eagles and buffaloes. These shirts were said to also make those who wore them safe from harm. The Army's bullets could not kill a Ghost Dancer who wore the magic shirt, Wovoka told them.

Wovoka said that Indians who danced the Ghost Dance would rise up into the sky while God covered the white man with a new earth. Then the Ghost Dancers would join their ancestors in a land filled with buffalo and game. The water would be sweet, the grass would be green, and there would be no white men.

So Native Americans danced and danced until they fainted. They paid no mind to the soldiers who were becoming alarmed at all of this "crazy" Indian dancing. The dancers believed the soldiers could not hurt them. Besides, Wovoka the

Messiah preached that the Indians should harm no one, should fight with no one. God alone would make the Native American ghosts rise.

Nevertheless, the U.S. government feared that an Indian uprising was about to happen. They decided to arrest one of the most important Sioux chiefs, Sitting Bull. Thousands of Sioux were joining the Ghost Dance movement. Although they were no longer fighting the U.S. Army, perhaps this Ghost Dancing might inspire them to fight—especially if Sitting Bull decided to lead them.

When the Indian police arrived to arrest Sitting Bull, he was willing to go quietly. However, when Sitting Bull and the police came out of Sitting Bull's cabin, they found a group of Ghost Dancers. The Ghost Dancers outnumbered the police by four to one. They shouted at the police that they could not take Sitting Bull. Catch-the-Bear, one of the dancers, pulled out his rifle and fired at the police. Now the promises of Wovoka would be tested. The Indians would learn whether the Ghost Shirts they wore had enough magic to stop the bullets of the white men.

This painting of the Trail of Tears depicts the grueling journey of the Cherokee through five states in 1838–39. At least one-third of the Indians forced to march to Indian Territory did not survive the journey.

2
THE TRAIL OF TEARS

AMERICA WAS THE "NEW WORLD" TO EUROPEANS, WHO SPOKE OF COLUMBUS "DISCOVERING" America as if the land did not exist until Europeans knew about it. Native Americans, however, had already inhabited America long before Columbus arrived. The Europeans still called them Indians, though long ago everyone figured out that Christopher Columbus had been mistaken when, in 1492, he arrived in America and thought he'd sailed around the world to India.

At the beginning of the 19th century, after America won its independence from Britain, more and more Europeans came to the United States. These new settlers wanted land. Although the Americans had made promises to Native Americans, as the demand for land grew, Americans did not keep their word.

For example, a law called the Northwest Ordinance of 1787 said that Indians' lands south of the Great Lakes would never be taken without their consent. It also said the European settlers would wage no wars against Indians. However, settlers ignored the rights of Indians, and soon Indians were fighting settlers. An alliance of Shawnee, Potawatomis, Ottawas, Ojibways, Delawares, and other tribes, led by a chief of the

Long before the United States became a country, colonists in North America had strained relations with the Native Americans. In this painting Algonquian Indians attack two English settlers who had wandered too far outside their settlement at Jamestown during the winter of 1610.

Miami tribe named Little Turtle, had some early victories. Soon, however, the chiefs realized they could not win. There were simply too many Europeans.

So Little Turtle and other chiefs took money from the U.S. government in exchange for land. The Treaty of Greenville in 1795 gave up much of Ohio and Indiana. However, not all Native

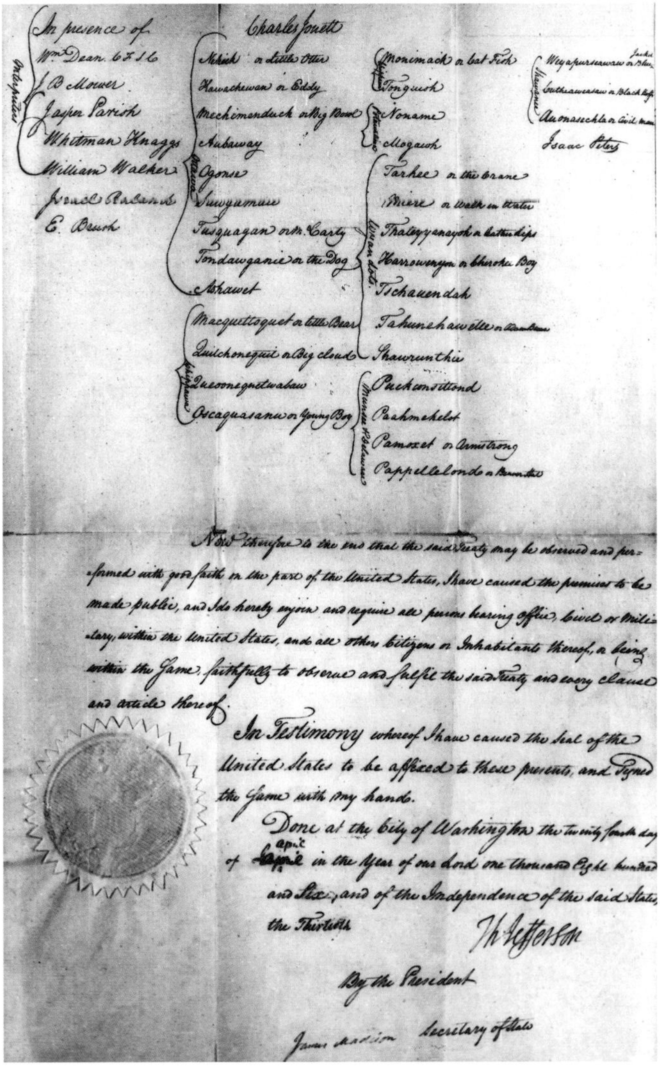

In presence of
Wm. Dean
J. B. Mower
Jasper Parish
Whitman Knaggs
William Walker
Isaac Paland
E. Brush

Charles Jouett
Nekeik or Little Otter
Kawachewan or Eddy
Mechimenduck or Big Bowl
Aubaway
Ogonse
Sawgamaw
Tusquagan or McCarty
Tondawganie or the Dog
Ashawet
Macquettoquet or Little Bear
Quitchonequit or Big cloud
Queonnequetwabaw
Oscaquasanu or Young Boy
Monimack or Cat Fish
Tonguish
Noname
Mogawh
Tarhee or the crane
Miere or Walk in water
Thateyyanayoh or Cuttendeps
Harrowenyou or Cherokee Boy
Tschauendah
Tahunehawette or Abandonia
Shawrunthie
Puckonsittond
Paahmehelot
Pamoxet or Armstrong
Pappellelond or Beaver Hat
Weyapurseawaw or Blue Jacket
Cutheaweasaw or Black Hoof
Auonaseckla or Civil man
Isaac Peters

Now therefore to the end that the said Treaty may be observed and performed with good faith on the part of the United States, I have caused the premises to be made public, and I do hereby enjoin and require all persons bearing office, civil or military, within the United States, and all other Citizens or Inhabitants thereof, or being within the same, faithfully to observe and fulfil the said Treaty and every clause and article thereof.

In Testimony whereof I have caused the Seal of the United States to be affixed to these presents, and signed the same with my hand.

Done at the City of Washington the twenty fourth day of April in the Year of our Lord one thousand Eight hundred and Six, and of the Independence of the said States, the Thirtieth.

Th: Jefferson

By the President

James Madison Secretary of State

This treaty between the United States and chiefs of the Ottawa, Chippawa, Potawatima, Wyamdot, Munsee of Delaware, and Shawnee tribes was signed by president Thomas Jefferson and his secretary of state, James Madison on April 24, 1806. Unfortunately, whites did not respect most of the treaties they negotiated with the Native Americans.

In 1824, the Bureau of Indian Affairs was created as a division in the War Department for the purpose of making treaties to speed up moving the Indian tribes westward.

Americans agreed that the chiefs could or should give up their lands to the European Americans. As the 19th century began, Indians differed in their views about the white man. Some thought they should adopt the ways of the white men and live alongside them. Others thought they should move west to escape the whites. And still others believed the tribes should stay on their lands and fight to defend them.

An event that shows the division among Native Americans took place in the Creek Indian War of 1813–14. The Creeks had already given up much of their land to the Americans, and a group of Creeks, called the "Red Sticks" and led by Chief Menawa, decided it was time to resist. General Andrew Jackson led an army of 3,300 men, including Cherokee and Creek Indians, against 1,000 Red Stick Creeks on March 27, 1814, at Horseshoe Bend in Alabama, killing more than 800 of them. In August of 1814, the Creeks were forced to sign a peace **treaty** giving the United States 23 million acres of land in Alabama and Georgia. Those signing this treaty included chiefs that had been **allies** with the U.S. Army against the Red Sticks.

As the Carolinas and Georgia filled with Europeans, some Native Americans decided they had little choice but to leave.

☛ William Clark had been co-leader of the Lewis and Clark expedition, which journeyed through the northwestern territories of the United States from 1804 to 1806. After returning from the wilderness, Clark became superintendent of Indian affairs, a position he held for 30 years. He also was governor of the Missouri Territory from 1813 to 1821.

The U.S. government had a place for them to go. William Clark, an Indian **superintendent** located in St. Louis, got some Osage chiefs to agree to share most of Arkansas and part of Missouri with the Cherokees. A group of Cherokees, led by Chief Tahlonteskee, gave up their lands in Georgia and went to live further west in the land of the Osages. The Osage chiefs agreed to this arrangement after being given pots, pans, beads, knives, and whiskey—a small price for so much land.

However, not only Cherokees but also white men hunting buffalo began to appear in the land of the Osages. The Osages got ready to make war. Instead, the U.S. government talked them into giving up even more land for the Cherokees.

Meanwhile, Andrew Jackson persuaded more Cherokees to sign treaties giving up their lands east of the Mississippi. By

Andrew Jackson was nicknamed "Sharp Knife" by the Indians.

1819, there were 6,000 Cherokee in Arkansas. Other eastern tribes had started moving west as well. In a treaty denounced as fraudulent by President John Quincy Adams, the Creek Indians agreed to be relocated in the West. Removal of the Indians westward was becoming the official policy of the United States.

On May 28, 1830, Andrew Jackson, now president of the United States, signed into law a bill for the complete removal of the Indians. The Cherokees who had remained in Georgia were stunned. They had tried to adopt the ways of the Europeans. They had even adopted a **constitution** modeled on the U.S. Constitution. Had they not been good neighbors?

However, the Americans had another reason for wanting the Cherokee lands in Georgia. Gold had been discovered there. The state of Georgia passed laws making it a crime to discourage Cherokees from leaving the state. When missionaries took the side of the Native Americans, they, too, were thrown in jail. The Cherokees would have to leave. The governor of Georgia divided up their territories and distributed it in a lottery to white Georgians.

Not all white Americans favored the removal of Native Americans. The Indians had some famous defenders in Congress, including Senator Daniel Webster and Senator Henry

Andrew Jackson was born March 15, 1767, on the border between North and South Carolina. At age 13, he joined the Continental Army as a messenger. After the Revolutionary War, Jackson decided to practice law in Nashville, Tennessee. He was elected a U.S. Senator and served as a Tennessee Supreme Court judge for six years.

Jackson was elected major general of the Tennessee militia and fought in the War of 1812, winning fame after his defeat of the British in the Battle of New Orleans. He earned the nickname "Old Hickory" because he ruled his troops strictly. He also led troops against the Seminole Indians in Florida and against the Creek Indians. He was elected president of the United States in 1828 and again in 1832. As president, he encouraged the Georgians to ignore Supreme Court rulings and force Indians in Georgia to relocate in Oklahoma. He retired from public life after his second term as president but remained active in politics behind the scenes. He died June 8, 1845.

Clay. In addition, Reverend Samuel Worcester, who was a missionary to the Cherokees in Georgia, went to court over Georgia's attempt to take Indian lands and won the case in the U.S. Supreme Court.

However, Georgia ignored the Supreme Court's ruling and so did President Andrew Jackson. The U.S. government

> Some of the Cherokees who signed the treaty eventually were killed by their own people because the Cherokees had passed a law saying that Cherokee chiefs who gave up land should be put to death.

began forcibly removing Indians. A few hundred Cherokees out of 17,000 signed the Treaty of New Echota in 1835. Even though almost all of the other Cherokees opposed the treaty, the U.S. government used these signatures to justify forced removal of the tribe.

About 3,000 Cherokees were sent on boats to "Indian Territory" in the West. During the winter of 1838–39, another 14,000 Indians were forced to march through Tennessee, Kentucky, Illinois, Missouri, and Arkansas. This event is known as the "Trail of Tears," because between 4,000 and 8,000 Indians died from hunger and illness.

Altogether, about 60,000 Indians were removed from the southeast United States. These included Cherokee, Choctaw, Creek, Chicksaw, and Seminole Indians. Since white Americans continued to move west as well, and Missouri had already become a state by 1821, Indian Territory needed to be even further west—Oklahoma.

The Native Americans who remained in the East were pressured to leave. Merchants sued them over phony debts and took their lands. The Indians couldn't defend themselves in court because laws had been passed prohibiting them from being legal witnesses. Even Indians that had been good neighbors and adopted the ways of the white man were driven west. This was a violation of the Indian Removal Act, which said that Indians could remain if they adopted white man ways. The white Americans simply wanted their lands, so their Native American neighbors were pushed to the west.

A few Cherokees managed to escape capture and hid in the mountains of North Carolina where their descendants still live today.

This 19th century drawing shows the Bad Axe Massacre, in which Sac and Fox Indians attempting to surrender were fired upon by whites aboard a steamboat. The massacre ended the Black Hawk War, which began when the Sac and Fox resisted being forced off their land.

3
THE BLACK HAWK WAR

THE SAC AND FOX TRIBES LIVED IN ILLINOIS AT THE BEGINNING OF THE 19TH CENTURY. THE SACS had built a settlement called Sacenuk where 11,000 Sacs lived.

These Native Americans had contact with whites through the fur trade. The Indians traded muskrat, beaver, and raccoon **pelts** for pots and pans, blankets, cloth, beads, guns, and knives. Over time, some of the chiefs went in debt to the whites and signed documents giving away parts of their land in exchange for canceling their debts. However, under the terms of these agreements, the Indians were not required to leave immediately.

In 1804, a Sac brave was arrested for killing three whites. The Sacs were told that the brave would not be released unless the Sacs signed a document giving up more land. After the Sac chiefs were given whiskey to drink, they signed the treaty. But instead of letting the Sac brave go, the whites shot him in the head. These Americans did not keep their promises, so during the War of 1812, the Sac and Fox tribes sided with the British.

In 1829, whites began to settle on the lands of the Sacs and Fox, purchasing from the government parts of the land that the Sacs and Fox had signed away. It was only then that

Lacrosse was a game played by Sacs and Fox as well as by other Native American tribes. In lacrosse, a netted racquet at the end of a stick is used to pick up, throw, and catch a ball. The object of the game is to get the ball into a goal. The word "lacrosse" was given to the game by French woodsmen, and refers to the curved stick, or cross, used in the game. The game later became popular among non-Indians. Today more than half a million people worldwide play lacrosse.

the Native Americans realized what had happened. They had given up their lands and were now ordered to leave.

Some of the Indians went west, to Iowa, but Black Hawk and his followers refused to leave. Black Hawk hoped that the

British would join him in an alliance, but the British told him that the Native Americans didn't have a chance against the Americans. Rather than have his people be killed by the white man's army, Black Hawk signed an agreement that required him and his people to go to Iowa and never come back to the east side of the Mississippi River.

It is said that when Black Hawk made his mark on the treaty, he pressed the quill against the paper so hard (out of anger) that he broke the pen.

However, after Black Hawk arrived in Iowa, he changed his mind. He decided that he and his people would return to plant corn. He thought the whites would leave him alone if he did no harm. Hearing rumors that Black Hawk was coming back, the whites began to raise an army.

In May of 1832, the army was approaching Black Hawk's camp. Believing the U.S Army was too big to defeat, Black Hawk sent messengers under a white flag, a sign of truce. However, the Americans ignored the white flag and killed the Indians.

When Black Hawk learned of this, he decided to take revenge. Leading a band of 40 warriors against 10 times as many American troops, Black Hawk drove the soldiers into retreat. However, Black Hawk knew that ultimately there were simply too many white soldiers for him to fight.

He and his followers made their way to southern Wisconsin. By now, they were running out of food, and they were reduced

The Army officer in charge of taking Black Hawk to St. Louis, where he would be imprisoned, was Jefferson Davis, the future president of the Confederacy.

to eating the bark off trees. Many of the older Sacs died of hunger. Some of them couldn't keep up the pace and had to be left behind. When whites found these older Native Americans, starving and helpless, they killed them.

Black Hawk and his people had to kill and eat most of their horses to keep from starving. Finally, they arrived at the Mississippi River at a place called Bad Axe. Many of Black Hawk's people had already died from hunger. When he saw a steamboat coming down the river, he raised a white flag. He told his warriors to put their guns down. He would surrender.

However, Black Hawk's attempt to surrender was met with cannon fire from the steamboat. White men on the steamboat began to shoot at the Sacs, killing about two dozen of them. After the steamboat had passed, a group of scouts from the American Army came upon the scene. Black Hawk again tried to surrender, but the scouts simply started shooting the Sacs. The American Army **massacred** women, children, and babies. Sac women were captured and raped by the American soldiers. Perhaps as many as 1,400 Sacs were killed. This event, on August 3, 1832, became known as the Bad Axe Massacre.

A few days later, Black Hawk surrendered to the

Black Hawk was born in 1767 in a Sac village at what is now Rock Island, Illinois. His name, Ma ka-tai-me-she-kia-kiak, meant Black Sparrow Hawk. The whites shortened his name to Black Hawk and eventually he started calling himself by the shorter name.

Black Hawk developed a reputation as a great warrior in battles against the Osage and Cherokee, and he became one of the most influential chiefs in the Sac and Fox. He opposed the actions of other chiefs who sold land to the whites. Black Hawk was given a silver medal of King George III in honor of his service to the British during the War of 1812. He wore the medal around his neck all the time. He was married to a woman named Singing Bird and they had many children.

After the Black Hawk War, he was taken on a tour of major cities in the eastern United States. He then was sent to his tribe's reservation in Iowa where he died in 1838. Before his death, he dictated an autobiography.

Winnebago tribe, who turned him over to the U.S. Army. Black Hawk was imprisoned but later released and taken back East. There he saw the cities of the white men and met Andrew Jackson. Then Black Hawk returned to the West and dictated his autobiography.

Native Americans depended on bison for many everyday necessities. No part of the slaughtered animal was wasted; the Indians ate the meat, used the bones to make tools and weapons, and used the hides to make clothing and shelter.

4

THE PUSH WEST

BY THE MID-1840S MOST OF THE NATIVE AMERICANS WHO HAD once lived east of the Mississippi River (at least 100,000) had been relocated in "Indian Territory." However, because so many white American settlers were also moving west, the boundaries of Indian Territory kept changing. The first Cherokees relocated to the west had shared land with the Osages in Arkansas and Missouri. Then, on June 30, 1834, Congress passed a law making Indian Territory that part of the land west of the Mississippi and not within Missouri, Louisiana, or Arkansas. Shortly after that, another law was passed to move the boundary of Indian Territory from the Mississippi River to the 95th **meridian**.

The Indians who were relocated had trouble finding enough food and water. They also had problems with the tribes who already were living in these lands. As the area became

How did the U.S. government justify taking land from Native Americans and breaking its promises? One way was what politicians called the doctrine of "Manifest Destiny." This doctrine said that Americans of European descent were a superior race, intended by fate or God to rule North America from the Atlantic to the Pacific, including the Indians and their land.

more crowded, native tribes and relocated tribes fought over hunting rights. Buffalo and other game became scarce. The government repeatedly reduced the size of Indian reservations. The land assigned to Indians as their reservation often wasn't suitable for farming. And then more white settlers arrived.

With the election of James K. Polk as president in 1845, America became even more committed to expanding the boundaries of the country. Texas was annexed as a state in 1845. Polk negotiated with the British to establish the northern border of the United States and solidify American claims to the Oregon Territory. When disputes arose with Mexico along the Texas frontier, Polk declared war against Mexico. When the war ended in 1848, the United States now owned even more territory—all the way from Texas to California. This could only mean trouble for the Indians.

When gold was discovered in California, thousands of Americans made their way across "Indian Territory" to seek gold. In 1850, California became a state, even though it was beyond the line of Indian Territory. White settlers who wanted

James Knox Polk was born November 2, 1795 in North Carolina. He practiced law and was elected to the Tennessee legislature and then to the U.S. House of Representatives. He was a good friend of Andrew Jackson during his presidency. After being elected governor of Tennessee, Polk ran for president of the United States, with strong support from Andrew Jackson, and was elected in 1845. During Polk's presidency, territory of the United States increased by more than a million square miles. When rumors of a gold strike in California were reported in1848, Polk told the nation that they were true, which encouraged many Americans to participate in the "gold rush." Polk did not run for a second term as president, and he died on June 15, 1849, only months after leaving office.

Indian land killed the Indians or chased them away. Native Americans forced off their lands sometimes starved or died of diseases like **smallpox**. If they raided mining camps to get food, the miners felt they had a good excuse to kill the Indians.

It became clear that Native Americans in the West would have to be put on reservations as well. In 1851 and 1852, Indians in California were pressured to sign treaties giving up land and agreeing to live on reservations. In return, the government also promised to provide the Indians with services and supplies. By 1853, according to the U.S. government, Native

Between 1848 and 1870, the number of Indians in California dropped from 150,000 to 30,000.

American tribes did not own land in California.

Similar events were occurring in other parts of the country. In Texas, white settlers fought with Comanches, Apaches, and Kiowas over control of the land. By the mid-1850s, the Indians were forced into two small reservations in northwest Texas. Gold was discovered in Colorado, drawing more settlers and **prospectors** to that area as well. To encourage settlement of Oregon and Washington, the United States offered large land grants to people willing to settle there. Then gold was discovered there as well, drawing even more settlers. The Indians of the Northwest would have to be confined to reservations, so that the white settlers and gold prospectors could take their land.

Some Indian lands were acquired by treaties with promises of money and services from the U.S. government. Other tribes resisted and went to war against the white settlers, and the Indians' lands were taken as they were defeated. Either way, by 1858, the northwest Indian tribes all were confined to reservations. That same year Minnesota became a state; its boundaries were only 100 miles west of the boundary line for "Indian Territory."

Thus, after only a few decades everyone realized that even though the United States had made a promise it to the

Indians, there would be no permanent Indian Territory. The United States now included California, Oregon, and Washington in the West and Texas to the south. More settlers were arriving in the Midwest. The Indians who remained in the Southwest and the Great Plains had reason to worry. It would only be a matter of time before they faced a choice between extermination and life on a reservation.

This oil painting depicts the Sand Creek Massacre, in which Arapaho and Cheyenne Indians were brutally attacked by American soldiers. The battle took place in their camp at Sand Creek in November 1864.

5

FIGHTING IN THE SOUTHWEST AND KANSAS

NEW MEXICO WAS NAVAHO COUNTRY. MANUELITO, A NAVAHO CHIEF, HAD MADE treaties with the whites. However, when the Army killed Navaho livestock because the animals came on pastures that the soldiers said belonged to them, the Navaho began to raid the Army's livestock and supply trains. Fighting grew worse, and after a Navaho attack on Fort Defiance on April 30, 1860, more soldiers were sent to the area to hunt down the Navaho warriors. The soldiers were unable to catch them, and both sides soon became weary of fighting. A peace treaty was signed in February of 1861.

General James Carleton arrived in New Mexico with his troops in the spring of 1862. Carleton had come to fight **Confederate** soldiers, but the Confederates had left the area. Carleton decided he would fight Indians instead. He ordered that no talks were to take place with the Native Americans

Chief Manuelito poses with a bow. The Navajo chief was involved in the skirmishes that led to the resettlement of Indians on a reservation at Bosque Redondo. Unsavory conditions caused the Indians to flee the reservation after a short time.

and that all Indian men were to be killed. Any survivors were to be sent to a reservation at Bosque Redondo.

First Carleton concentrated on the Mescalero Apaches. By spring of 1863, most of them had been killed, fled the country, or had been relocated on the reservation. Now Carleton turned his attention to the Navahos. He gave them until July 20 to give themselves up but none did. Carleton grew impatient.

Kit Carson and soldiers under his command began to destroy all of the crops and livestock of the Navaho. In October, some of the Navahos surrendered and were sent to Bosque Redondo. During the early months of 1864, Kit Carson and his men pursued the Navahos in their mountain hideouts. The Navahos were starving, and within a few months, many more had surrendered. They were marched to Bosque Redondo in freezing weather and snowstorms. Hundreds died along the way. By the spring of 1864, around 8,500 Apaches and Navahos had been sent to the reservation.

Relations between the U.S. Army and the Navahos took a turn for the worse in the fall of 1861 because of a horse race between chief Manuelito and one of the soldiers. Many bets had been placed on the race, but Manuelito lost control of his horse because someone had cut his bridle rein. The Navaho, angry at being cheated, tried to force their way into the fort and fighting broke out. Many Navahos, including women and children, were massacred.

Those who made it to Bosque Redondo may have wished they hadn't. They did not have enough clothing, food, blankets, or firewood. The 1864 crops at Bosque failed, and starvation and disease killed many of the Navahos. Those who could escaped. So many were fleeing the reservation that by the fall of 1865, Carleton ordered that every Navaho found off the reservation should be killed. The crops at Bosque failed again in 1865, and the Indians were given food that had been found unfit for soldiers to eat. More Indians died.

Manuelito finally surrendered in the fall of 1866. Soon after that, a new superintendent was appointed for the reservation and declared it unfit for living. New reservation lands were given to the Indians closer to their old homes.

When Kit Carson was first ordered to prepare for war against the Navahos, he resigned. He had been friendly with the Indians and had lived with them for months. He also had a child by an Indian woman. However, Carson later withdrew his resignation and prepared to fight the Navahos.

In 1858, gold was discovered in Colorado. Once again the U.S. government decided to take away Indian land that had been given to Native Americans in a treaty that had been signed only seven years earlier. Some Cheyennes and Arapahos agreed to sign the treaty when they were told it guaranteed them freedom of movement for hunting. Only six of their 44 chiefs signed this treaty, however.

Between gold prospectors, settlers, and U.S. soldiers, it became harder for the Indians to avoid contact with the whites. In May of 1864, hearing that soldiers were nearby, Cheyenne chief Lean Bear and some warriors went to see what they wanted. Lean Bear approached them by himself. When he was about 20 yards away, the soldiers fired on him and killed him. Fighting broke out, but Chief Black Kettle persuaded his people to stop fighting. Black Kettle sent a message through a friendly white man that he did not want any more fighting. However, the governor of Colorado already had decided that peace was not an option.

Black Kettle and other chiefs met with U.S. Army officers. They were told they must surrender. Soon after that Black Kettle and his followers made their way to Sand Creek, 40

☛ Kit Carson was a reluctant, though highly effective, Indian fighter. Using merciless tactics to rid the area of Native Americans, he helped to change the face of the Southwest.

miles from Fort Lyon, and sent messengers to visit with the commander there. The Arapahos with Black Kettle moved down by the fort and began receiving **rations** from the Army. Black Kettle's Cheyennes stayed at Sand Creek. Everything seemed fine.

Then the commander at Fort Lyon was replaced by Major Scott J. Anthony. Major Anthony demanded surrender of the Arapahos' weapons. Then he told Black Kettle that as long as the Cheyenne stayed at Sand Creek, they would be safe. However, Anthony had sent for reinforcements. He planned to massacre Black Kettle and the Cheyenne.

There were about 600 Indians camped at Sand Creek the morning of November 29, 1864, two-thirds of them women

This colored postcard shows a studio portrait of the only survivor of the Sand Creek Massacre. The young Arapaho girl was orphaned by the violent attack; she was later raised by a white family.

and children. The Indians were flying an American flag, a gift from an officer who promised they would be safe as long as they flew the flag. The soldiers of Major Anthony and Colonel John Chivington attacked. Women and children were slaughtered. Bodies were mutilated. Fortunately, many of the Native Americans, including Black Kettle, were able to escape, but the Army killed 133 Indians, more than 100 of them women and children.

The Sand Creek Massacre ruined any chance of peace. Cheyenne, Arapaho, and Sioux began attacking wagon trains and small military posts. They destroyed telegraphs and killed white settlers. However, they knew they could not go back. They would have to flee Colorado. Most of them decided to go north to join the Teton Sioux and the Northern Cheyenne. Black Kettle and his followers went to live south of the Arkansas River.

Though they had been driven out of Colorado, technically the Indians still owned the land. On October 14, 1865, Black Kettle and other chiefs agreed to sign a treaty giving up legal ownership of their lands in Colorado. Meanwhile, Congress continued to encourage white settlers to come to what once had been Indian Territory. Before the Civil War, as many as 50,000 settlers passed through Fort Laramie in a single year. The Homestead Act was passed in 1862, giving settlers 160 acres in Kansas and Nebraska, even though legally the Indians possessed the land.

In June of 1864, John Evans, governor of Colorado ordered all "friendly" Indians to report to Fort Lyon. In August, the governor authorized Colorado citizens to kill and destroy all "hostile" Indians (ones who had not surrendered).

The Indian chief Roman Nose returned to Kansas in the spring of 1866 to hunt, even though chiefs had given these lands by treaty to the whites. Roman Nose had just won a great victory in Powder River country, and the Southern Cheyennes and Arapahos looked to him as a leader. When a **stagecoach** line was opened that, like the wagon trains, ran straight through the best buffalo ranges, Roman Nose and his warriors told the company they would start raiding if the stagecoaches continued. Then Roman Nose settled into camp to wait for spring.

However, soldiers led by General Winfield Scott Hancock were soon headed for Kansas. Hancock demanded that Roman Nose meet with him, but Roman Nose refused. Finally, Hancock marched troops to Roman Nose's camp. Roman Nose sent the women and children away, met with Hancock, and promised to bring his people back to their camp. However, he and his warriors escaped. Hancock sent troops to Roman Nose's abandoned camp and destroyed everything there.

In revenge, Roman Nose and his warriors raided stagecoach stations, attacked railroads, and ripped out telegraph lines. However, other Indians submitted to the U.S. Army and were sent to reservations.

In 1868, General Philip Sheridan took command of soldiers

The real name for the American buffalo is bison. Nearly 4 million bison were killed between 1872 and 1874, but only 150,000 of them by Native Americans. Buffalo Bill Cody was famous for killing buffalo—allegedly more than 4,000 in about a year and a half. Native Americans used every bit of the buffalos they killed, including their bones and meat, but white settlers killed buffalo just for their hides. Then, realizing that Indians couldn't live without the buffalo, white men started killing the animals as a strategy to destroy the Indians.

in Kansas's forts and tried to hunt down Roman Nose and his band of about 300 warriors. In the fall of 1868, at the battle of Beecher's Island, Roman Nose was killed. His death was a great blow to the Indians. They did not know that General Sheridan planned to massacre the peaceful Indians who had not followed Roman Nose.

On November 27, 1868, Lieutenant Colonel George A. Custer and the Seventh Calvary attacked Black Kettle's camp on the Washita River. Custer had orders to destroy the village and kill the warriors. Black Kettle had escaped the massacre at Sand Creek, but he could not escape this one. Soldiers killed 103 Cheyennes, but only 11 of them were warriors. The village was destroyed and hundreds of Indian ponies were slaughtered. The survivors surrendered at Fort Cobb in December. Although a few Cheyenne warriors continued to resist under the leadership of Tall Bull, they were captured or killed in 1869.

In Arizona, bands of Apaches led by Cochise and Mangas Coloradas were resisting the Army. When Mangus rode into an Army camp that had hoisted a white flag to negotiate peace, the soldiers captured him, tortured him, and killed him.

For a few years, Cochise continued to lead a band of about

Cochise had welcomed the white men to his country until he and his family were arrested and falsely accused of a crime. Cochise escaped but the U.S. soldiers murdered his family.

General Philip Sheridan was a hero of the Civil War. After the war, he led the U.S. Army in its fight against the western Native American tribes. Sheridan was once quoted as saying, "The only good Indians I ever saw were dead." However, Sheridan denied ever making the statement.

300 warriors in raids. Cochise could not be captured, but innocent Indians could be punished. Tucson citizens formed a **posse** and massacred a village of Apaches near Camp Grant, raping and mutilating. Many of the 144 victims were women and babies. President Grant called the massacre "purely murder," but a Tucson jury set the killers free.

A peace treaty was made with Cochise allowing him and his followers to live at a certain place, but after a few months the government tried to move them again. Cochise went back to warfare. Another treaty was signed in the summer of 1873. Cochise died the next year of illness.

By the spring of 1875, most Apaches were on reservations or hiding in Mexico. One of the Apache leaders in Mexico was

Geronimo. Captured in March of 1877, he was held for four months by the U.S. Army and then released.

During the following years, Apaches who did not want to be forced to live on reservations raided Mexicans and Americans alike as part of Geromino's war party. By 1882, the United States had an agreement with Mexico that allowed them to come into Mexico to capture hostile Apaches. Then Geronimo reached an agreement with General Crook in 1884, and the Apaches returned to the reservation. In 1885, however, Geronimo and others left the reservation and rcturned to Mexico. Finally, another surrender was negotiated. Geronimo, the last Apache chief, died a prisoner of war at Fort Sill, Oklahoma, in 1909.

Many whites considered Indians less than human. In an 1879 court case, a U.S. district attorney even argued that court orders requiring the release of the person Standing Bear did not have to be obeyed because Indians were not persons.

The members of George Custer's Seventh Cavalry attempt to hold off an overwhelming force of Native Americans during the battle of the Little Bighorn, June 25, 1876. Although the battle was a great victory for the Sioux and Cheyenne, it would turn out to be one of their last triumphs against the U.S. Army.

6

THE GREAT PLAINS

THE LARGEST WESTERN TRIBE WAS THE SIOUX. THE TRIBE WAS DIVIDED INTO DIFFERENT groups. The Santee Sioux lived in the woodlands of Minnesota. The Teton Sioux lived on the Great Plains along with the Cheyennes and other tribes.

The Santee Sioux had been dealing with the white men for some time. Treaties had been signed in which 90 percent of Santee land had been given to the whites. During the decade before the Civil War more than 150,000 whites had settled in Santee country. The Santees were in debt, their crops had failed, most of the game was gone from the reservation lands, and traders had cheated them.

When money due the Santees didn't arrive in the summer of 1862, they were unable to buy food. Their people were starving. On August 4, 1862, 500 desperate Santees stormed a warehouse. A fight was avoided and the U.S. agent promised Chief Little Crow that food would be released to the Santees from another warehouse 30 miles away.

However, the traders at the other warehouse would not issue food on credit. The Santees were very angry. Then, a few days later, a few hotheaded Santees killed some white settlers.

The Santees expected that all the Indians would be punished for this deed and decided to strike first.

The Santees, led by Little Crow, killed 20 men and took the food from the storehouse. Then they attacked Fort Ridgely and the town of New Ulm. The Santee braves killed hundreds of settlers along the Minnesota River. By this time, Minnesota's Governor Alexander Ramsey had announced to the citizens of Minnesota that "the Sioux Indians must be exterminated or forever driven beyond the borders of this state."

The Army sent troops commanded by Colonel Henry Sibley. The Santee chiefs decided they were not strong enough to defeat Sibley and his men. Either they would have to surrender or leave to live with the Teton Sioux on the Great Plains. Little Crow decided to live with the Plains Indians. He would be killed later when he returned to Minnesota to steal horses.

About 2,000 Santees remained when Sibley marched into their camp and demanded their surrender. The 600 adult males were chained together and put in prison. Then they were sent to court (without attorneys), and 303 were sentenced to death. Before executing them, General John Pope sent the cases to President Abraham Lincoln for his approval. Lincoln had the cases reviewed and found only 39 cases were sufficient to merit a hanging.

The government took the remaining lands of the Santees, and the Santees were sent to live at a reservation on Crow Creek in the Dakota Territory. The soil there was poor, there was no game, and the water was bad. About 300 of the 1,300 Santee sent there in 1863 died during the first winter.

West of the Black Hills of the Dakotas, in Wyoming and Montana, was Powder River country. This was the stronghold of the Teton Sioux. Cheyenne and Arapaho were living there, too. The Indians in Powder River country felt safe and were surprised when U.S. soldiers decided to invade.

The Cheyenne chief Roman Nose prepared to fight the white man by lying on a raft in a lake, praying to the Great Medicine Man and to the water spirits. Then an old medicine man made him a war bonnet to protect him from harm.

In July of 1865, General Patrick E. Connor announced that all the Indians north of the Platte River should be "hunted down like wolves." He ordered his soldiers to attack and kill all male Indians more than 12 years of age. Connor organized three groups of soldiers to invade Powder River country. One group, led by him, constructed a fort that he named after himself. Then he took part of his troops and surprised a group of Arapahos, destroying their village and capturing a third of their ponies.

However, the other two groups of soldiers he had organized were in another part of Powder River country. They were weak from the march, low on food, and sick. There wasn't enough grass and water for their horses. A group of Sioux with Chief Sitting Bull came upon this second group in September

Sitting Bull had a vision after three days of dancing the sun dance. He saw soldiers falling from the sky and said the Great Spirit was giving these soldiers to the Indians to kill.

of 1865. When Indians rode into the Army camp under a flag of truce, the soldiers shot and killed many of them.

Sitting Bull realized, though, that the soldiers' horses were half-starved, and he decided to attack, even though there were only 400 Sioux against 2,000 soldiers. The Indians drove them south. When a sleet storm struck, the soldiers' horses could go no further. The soldiers shot their horses and continued on foot, but they were finally trapped and surrounded.

The Indian Roman Nose now asked to lead a charge against the soldiers. He told his warriors not to charge until he, Roman Nose, had made them empty their guns shooting at him. Then Roman Nose rode his horse directly at the line of soldiers. When he was close enough to see their faces, he rode from one end of the soldiers' line to the other and back again as they fired at him but could not kill him. Finally, when they shot his horse out from under him, the other warriors charged.

During the first part of 1866, the government tried to get the important Sioux warrior chief Red Cloud to sign a treaty at Fort Laramie. For a while, the Indians negotiated, but on June 13, 1866, another regiment of soldiers arrived at Fort Laramie. Red Cloud was outraged. As Red Cloud left, he said,

"Great Father sends us presents and wants new road. But White Chief goes with soldiers to steal road before Indians says yes or no!"

In July of 1866, Red Cloud and his warriors attacked. Throughout the summer of 1866 they continued to skirmish with the soldiers. On December 21, 1866, Red Cloud's warriors, including Crazy Horse, drew the soldiers out of Fort

The bravery of Roman Nose earned him the respect of his tribe. During one battle, he rode ahead of his men to draw fire from the U.S. soldiers; after the soldiers had emptied their rifles at the chief, his warriors charged the army encampment.

Unlike other famous Indian warriors, Crazy Horse never let anyone photograph him.

Phil Kearny. Soldiers under the command of Captain William Fetterman pursued them. It was a trap. Indians appeared from either side and killed all 81 of the soldiers. Although the Indians lost more men that day than the Army, "Fetterman's Massacre," as it became known, made a big impression on the U.S. government. It was the worst defeat that Indians had ever inflicted on the U.S. Army to that point.

Red Cloud demanded that the soldiers leave Powder River country or he would not sign a treaty. Finally, the government ordered that the forts in Powder River country be abandoned. The troops at Fort C. F. Smith left on July 29, 1868. The next morning a group of warriors led by Red Cloud burned it down. The other forts were abandoned also, and on November 6, 1868, Red Cloud signed the treaty.

The Indians could not read, though, and the Army lied about what the treaty said, as the Indians would find out later. The treaty required them to trade in another part of the country, which would have caused them to have to move from the area.

However, for a time, things seemed to be getting better for the Indians. The U.S. government even appointed a Native American named Ely Parker to be Commissioner of Indian Affairs. Parker managed to smooth over disputes between Red

Cloud and the government. Unfortunately, people in Washington less friendly toward the Indians soon forced Parker out of his job.

The battle at Little Bighorn is known as "Custer's Last Stand."

When gold was discovered in the Black Hills of South Dakota, the government decided once again to send troops to Sioux territory under the command of George Custer. By the spring of 1875, gold prospectors were swarming the Black Hills. The U.S. Army was supposed to keep the prospectors off Indian land but the soldiers didn't enforce the law. Instead, the U.S. government wanted to buy the land. When

Red Cloud was the leader of one of the most devastating Indian attacks against the U.S. Army, in which Captain William Fetterman and the 80 men under his command were killed. The Sioux warrior chief led a successful war against the United States from 1866 to 1868, which was finally ended by the Treaty of Fort Laramie—a treaty the United States violated within a few months.

George Armstrong Custer was born in Ohio in 1839. He grew up in Michigan and attended school at West Point, graduating last in his class. However, he was successful as an officer during the Civil War, fighting in many battles. After the Civil War, Custer went west to fight Indians. In 1876, he was chosen to lead an expedition against the Sioux. He is best known for his last battle, in which Sitting Bull and Crazy Horse defeated him at the Little Bighorn.

Red Cloud wouldn't sell, the U.S. government used the same tactics it had before: they ordered all Indians to report to their reservations, while troops hunted down "hostile" Indians.

Though Red Cloud had dealt with the U.S. government in the past, by this time Sitting Bull had become the big chief of the Sioux, and the Sioux's greatest warrior was Crazy Horse. Troops commanded by General Crook attacked several thousand Sioux camped with Sitting Bull and Crazy Horse at the Rosebud River and were defeated. The Indians then moved their camp to the Little Bighorn River in Montana Territory.

On June 25, 1876, Custer and his troops arrived at the Little Bighorn. The Indians were attacked by Custer from one side and by Major Reno from the other. However, the army quickly was forced to retreat. The Indians killed Custer and all of his men and trapped Reno and his men. When the Indians heard that more troops were coming, they left the area to avoid further fighting.

The father and mother of Crazy Horse are said to have taken his heart and bones and buried them somewhere near the creek called Wounded Knee.

The U.S. government decided to punish the innocent Indians who had remained on their reservations. These Indians, who had done nothing, were declared prisoners of war. Then a law was passed that took from the Indians all rights to Powder River country and the Black Hills, even though this violated previous treaties made with the Sioux.

In April of 1877, his warriors starving, Crazy Horse agreed to surrender because the government promised him a reservation in Powder River country. However, when he turned himself in and saw they were going to chain him and put him in a jail cell, he resisted and a soldier killed him with a **bayonet** on September 5, 1877.

As of 1990, about 2 million Native Americans lived in North America, a little over a third of them on or near reservations.

Sitting Bull would not surrender. In 1877 he decided to flee to Canada. However, he and his people did not own the land there. By July 19, 1881, Sitting Bull had returned, and he and his remaining followers surrendered.

The government began passing laws in the 1880s and 1890s that

Chief Big Foot, the leader of the Sioux after the death of Sitting Bull, lies frozen in the snow at Wounded Creek. Big Foot was shot through the head. The massacre at Wounded Knee marked the end of Native American uprisings against the United States.

made the practice of Indian religions a crime. Those who did could be jailed or lose their rations. However, they Indian ways could not be entirely suppressed.

In 1890, the Ghost Dance became popular among Native Americans. The Indians believed that the ghosts of Indians would return and a new world, in which only Indians lived, would appear. The religion made the U.S. government nervous. When Indian police surrounded Sitting Bull's cabin on December 15, 1890 to arrest him, the Ghost Dancers' efforts proved to be in vain. Shots were fired and Sitting Bull was killed.

On December 29, 1890, a group of Sioux led by Chief Big Foot was camped at Wounded Knee under the watch of the U.S. Army. The army required that all weapons be surrendered, and the Sioux complied. However, one Indian did not want to give up his expensive rifle. When a gunshot

Sitting Bull was born in South Dakota around 1831. His nickname was "Slow" because he always took his time. He fought in his first war party at age 14 and soon became known for his courage. Around 1867, Sitting Bull became the main chief of the Sioux. He was considered a wise and effective leader, and he increased the hunting grounds of the Sioux. When gold was discovered in the Dakotas and Army troops returned, Sitting Bull and Crazy Horse scored some important victories against the Army, especially "Custer's Last Stand," the battle at Little Bighorn. However, the U.S. Army was too strong for Sitting Bull and his followers to defeat, so they went to Canada. Unable to survive there, they returned in 1881 and Sitting Bull surrendered. In 1885, Sitting Bull joined Buffalo Bill's Wild West show and traveled around the U.S. and Canada. Sitting Bull was killed while being arrested during the Ghost Dance craze in 1890.

sounded, the soldiers opened fire. Since the Indians had few weapons, they could not fight back. Between 153 and 300 of the 350 Sioux were killed.

This event became known as the Wounded Knee Massacre. It brought the end of the Ghost Dance movement. The disillusioned Native Americans gave up all hope. They at last accepted that they could no longer fight against the white men's broken promises.

GLOSSARY

Allies
Groups or nations who are friends, offering support to each other during a war.

Bayonet
A steel blade attached to the muzzle end of a shoulder arm (like a rifle), used in hand-to-hand combat.

Confederate
The group of southern states that dropped out of the Union and fought the North during the Civil War.

Constitution
The written laws and basic principles of a nation or social group, determining the powers and duties of the government and guaranteeing certain rights to the people.

Massacre
The act of brutally killing helpless or unresisting people.

Meridian
An imaginary east-west line on the globe used to measure longitude.

Messiah
A savior.

Parley
A conference or discussion between enemies.

Pelts
Animal skins, hides.

Posse
A group summoned by a sheriff to assist in preserving the peace.

Prospectors
Explorers who search mineral deposits such as gold and silver.

Rations

Food allowances.

Reservation

Land set aside by the U.S. government on which Native Americans are expected to live.

Smallpox

A contagious disease; one symptom was "poxes," skin eruptions like large pimples that left deep scars.

Stagecoach

A horse-drawn passenger and mail vehicle that ran on a regular schedule between established stops.

Superintendent

A person who oversees or is in charge.

Treaty

A written agreement or contract.

Truce

A pause in fighting, a cease-fire.

TIMELINE

1814
On March 27, Andrew Jackson and troops kill 800 Red Stick Creeks at Horseshoe Bend in Alabama. In August, the Creeks sign a treaty giving up 23 million acres of land in Georgia and Alabama.

1824
The Bureau of Indian Affairs is created as part of the War Department.

1828
Andrew Jackson is elected President.

1830
The Indian Removal Act is signed into law on May 28.

1832
The Bad Axe Massacre occurs on August 3, ending the Blackhawk War.

1835
The treaty of New Echota is ratified, though most Cherokee oppose it.

1838–1839
Cherokees are relocated to Indian Territory; thousands die on the "Trail of Tears."

1845
James K. Polk is elected president. Expansion into Indian territories will be encouraged.

1848
The United States wins the war against Mexico, acquiring more land from Texas to California.

1849

The California Gold Rush begins, causing prospectors and settlers to want Indian land. By 1853, Indian title to land in California has been eliminated.

1862

The Homestead Act is passed, giving 160 acres to settlers, even if the land is Indian land.

1862

Little Crow leads the Santee Sioux against the Army, but must flee to the Great Plains. The remaining Santee are sent to reservations.

1864

Kit Carson and General James Carleton end Navaho resistance and the Navahos march to their reservation.

1864

On November 29, members of the Cheyenne tribe are massacred at Sand Creek. Indians flee Colorado and in a few months sign a treaty giving up claims to land in Colorado.

1868

Red Cloud drives U.S. troops out of Powder River country; on November 26, Custer's Seventh Calvary slaughters Black Kettle and many women and children near Fort Cobb.

1876

Custer is defeated at Little Bighorn on June 25. However, the U.S. Army is too strong for the Sioux. During the following years the Sioux surrender.

1890

The Wounded Knee Massacre on December 29 brings an end to Native American resistance.

FURTHER READING

Bealer, Alex W. *Only the Names Remain: The Cherokees and the Trail of Tears*. New York: Little, Brown, 1996.

Brown, Dee. *Bury My Heart at Wounded Knee, An Indian History of the American West*. New York: Henry Holt, 1970.

Bruchac, Joseph. *A Boy Called Slow: The True Story of Sitting Bull*. New York: Paper Star, 1998.

Buchanan, John. *Jackson's Way: Andrew Jackson and the People of the Western Waters*. New York: John Wiley, 2001.

Coleman, William S. E. *Voices of Wounded Knee*. Lincoln: University of Nebraska Press, 2000.

Diessner, Don. *There Are No Indians Left but Me! Sitting Bull's Story*. Boca Raton, Fla.: Upton, 1993.

Ehle, John. *The Trail of Tears: The Rise and Fall of the Cherokee Nation*. Landover Hills, Md.: Anchor, 1989.

Hittman, Michael. *Wovoka and the Ghost Dance*. Lincoln: University of Nebraska Press, 1998.

Jahoda, Gloria. *The Trail of Tears*. San Antonio, Tex.: Wings Press, 1995.

McCormick, Anita Louise. *Native Americans and the Reservation in American History*. Springfield, N.J.: Enslow, 1996.

McClerran, Alice. *The Ghost Dance*. New York: Clarion, 1995.

Mooney, James. *The Ghost Dance Religion and the Sioux Outbreak of 1890*. Lincoln: University of Nebraska Press, 1991.

Stewart, Frank. *River Rising: A Cherokee Odyssey*. Ventura Calif.: Wohali Press, 1998.

Sullivan, Mark T. *Ghost Dance*. New York: Harper, 2000.

Utley, Robert. *The Lance and the Shield: The Life and Times of Sitting Bull*. New York: Ballantine, 1994.

Wilson, James. *The Earth Shall Weep, A History of Native America* New York: Atlantic Monthly Press, 1998.

INTERNET RESOURCES

Treaties between the United States and Native Americans

http://www.yale.edu/lawweb/avalon/ntreaty/ntreaty.htm

http://collections.ic.gc.ca/treaties/code/

http://www.rootsweb.com/~usgenweb/wa/indians/treaties.htm

The battle of the Little Bighorn

http://www.nps.gov/libi/

Error! Reference source not found.

http://www.custer-sd.com/

The Cherokee Trail of Tears

http://www.ngeorgia.com

http://rosecity.net/tears/trail/tearsnht.html

http://www.smokymtnmall.com/mall/cindians.html

Indian Wars in the West

Error! Reference source not found.

http://www.americanwest.com/pages/indians.htm

http://www.theoldwestwebride.com/txt7/inbios.html

http://www.colorado.edu/AmStudies/lewis/2010/indians.htm

http://www.virtualology.com/americanwest/

Sitting Bull

http://www.incwell.com/Biographies/SittingBull.html

http://www.theoldwestwebride.com/txt7/inbios2.html#anchor1744808

http://www.intuitive.com/sites/cbhma/sitbull-bio.html

INDEX

PHOTO CREDITS

2: Denver Public Library
6-7: Hulton/Archive
10: The Woolaroc Museum
12: National Park Service, Colonial National Historical Park
13: Hulton/Archive
15: Independence National Historical Park, Philadelphia
17: Independence National Historical Park, Philadelphia
20-21: Hulton/Archive
22: Hulton/Archive
25: Hulton/Archive
26-27: North Wind Picture Archives
29: Bettmann/Corbis
32-33: Colorado Historical Society
34: Denver Public Library
37: Courtesy Museum of New Mexico, neg. no. 45968
38: Denver Public Library
42: Corbis
44-45: Little Bighorn Battlefield National Monument/National Park Service
49: Denver Public Library
51: Denver Public Library
52: West Point Museum Collection/U.S. Military Academy
54: National Archives

Cover photos:
(front) The Woolaroc Museum
(back) Denver Public Library

ABOUT THE AUTHOR

Mike Wilson has published numerous articles on history in magazines for children. He also has written instructional material for Harcourt Brace and will have a biography of Father Roy Bourgois published by John Gordon Burke Publishers. He is also the author of *The Conquest of Mexico* in Mason Crest Publishers' EXPLORATION AND DISCOVERY series.